GERMANY

The most beautiful places and regions

SCHÖNING VERLAG

SCHÖNING GmbH & CO KG
An der Hülshorst 5 · 23568 LÜBECK
☎ (04 51) 31 03-0 · Fax: (04 51) 3 52 83
E-mail: info@schoening-verlag.de
Internet: www.schoening-verlag.de
ISBN: 978-3-89917-457-1
6th edition

Germany is beautiful ...

and we want to show it to you. Where fog rises over the Elbe, the Dresden Striezelmarkt glitters in the bright lights or the evening sun makes the vines on the Mosel gleam gold, it is then that Germany is simply a feast for the eyes.

This country in the heart of Europe offers tourists a very wide range of landscapes. Its regions include the "Wattenmeer" mud flats, the barren Rhone, the Ruhr, long since "green again", and the Lausitz lake landscape. Embedded among them we find the tourist highlights that all the world knows about and wants to see: fairytale King Ludwig's castles in Bavaria and the Holstentor in Lübeck, the Dresden Zwinger and the medieval lanes of Rothenburg, the Loreley on the Rhine and the chalky cliffs of Rügen. But in between you'll find a great deal of unknown Germany: the beavers dwelling in the river meadowlands of the Oder, the eagles soaring over Berchtesgaden National Park and the bee-eaters nesting on the sunny slopes of the Kaiserstuhl. There are remote lakes like the Maare in the Eifel, lonely mountain chains in the Allgäu Alps, over which the wind alone wafts, and moors around Bremen, on which a hiker only very occasionally loses his way. And who knows offhand that a quarter of the area of the industrial country of Germany is designated as natural park?

Germany also boasts countless historical monuments bearing witness to a great cultural tradition. You could mention Maulbronn Monastery, Roman Trier or the Wieskirche – 33 places and buildings have already been declared part of the UNESCO world cultural heritage. Only a few people know that the Eisenhütte in Völklingen, Bauhaus in Dessau and Zeche Zollverein in Essen are among them. And who knows the no less remarkable moated castles in Münsterland, the impressive brick buildings of Stralsund and the various objects that the art exhibition documenta leaves behind every four years in Kassel?

Germany lives fast, no doubt about it. In Berlin, Hamburg and Düsseldorf, everybody is on the go, well aware of the international

trends and often setting them themselves. But in the banking metropolis of Frankfurt, also pensioners chat calmly over cider, lovers stroll absorbed in one another through the Herrenhausen Gardens of the EXPO city of Hanover, and in the beer gardens of the cosmopolitan city of Munich quite a few seasoned car managers sometimes forget the time pressure and indulge in another 'Maß" (two pints).

But, last by no means least, Germany is simply loveable. Take its different dialects. Or its culinary delicacies ranging from Allgäuer Kässpatzen (cheese pasta) to Cologne's Halve Hahn (cheese roll). And also the Germans, whether the shrimpers in Büsum or the woman baker in the Swabian Alb, the Oberammergau Hergottschnitzer carvers or the waitress at the Bremer Schlachte – there are countless people in Germany who willingly help strangers and enjoy showing them more of their part of the country.

Not to mention fire brigade festivities, Corpus Christi processions, fisherfolk festivals. How much and how cheerfully the Germans celebrate! The beer flows in Magdeburg as in Passau, the glasses of wine sparkle in Freiberg and Cochem, where visitors are always warmly welcome. And when students from all over the world celebrate on a summer night in Göttingen, or exulting Japanese tourists in Heidelberg Castle never put their cameras away, well, then Germany is a particularly wonderful place. It's obvious that today it is closely connected with its neighbours and the world. It has become truly international.

Elegant and simple, dynamic and peaceful, stylish and down-to-earth – Germany is all these things. It's high time to take a much closer look at this fascinating country.

The North Sea – tides and romantic lighthouses

▲ Westerhever Lighthouse
◀ Walk across the mud flats at low tide

A wind is nearly always blowing from the west. It ruffles the water or churns it up into deep waves, wafts over the heavy black soil of the marshland, where cabbage flourishes as nowhere else, and over the hills of the coastal sandy moorland, left behind by the glaciers of the Ice Age. The sea sets the pace of life here. In a rhythm of about six hours, it rises and falls between two and three metres – that is the turn of the tide. When the water recedes, the Watt, the oozy, black grey seabed, is laid bare and it's time for a walk across the mudflats. Seaweed pops underfoot; a pair of stranded jellyfish dry out on the sand; millions of sea creatures, sandworms, hermit crabs, soft-shell clams, develop in tideways and channels.

Pied avocets and oyster fishers help themselves from this well-stocked larder and breed in the shore area. The Wattenmeer stretching from the Netherlands up to Denmark, covering 525,000 ha, was thus declared a National Park in 1986.

For centuries, people have tried to protect the land with dykes against the onslaught of the sea. But in great storm floods the North Sea has continually claimed back entire coastal strips, torn away entire localities and beaches, leaving behind tens of thousands of dead. Yet the people remained, fishing, going out to sea, hunting whales, growing grain and plundering ships that had run aground. Today visitors are received in friendlier style – with a cup of tea or a "Pharisäer", similar to Irish coffee. And they find plenty to admire in East Frisia, Dithmarschen and North Frisia: the Henry Nannen Art Museum in Emden, the Mill Museum in Aurich, the nature reserves on Juist, Baltrum and Spiekeroog. You can sample beer in Jever, go out to sea in the shrimp boats in Büsum. And in the Cuxhaven Wreck Museum you can also find out about the grim side of life on the coast.

▲ Seals

▲ Fishing cutter

▼ Typical Frisian house

Red Sand Lighthouse ▶

Free Hanseatic City of Bremen

▲ Town hall and cathedral

In the market square, the ten-metre high Roland watches over the independence of the city, as it has done for six centuries. International restaurants are lined up one after the other on the Schlachte, the lively promenade on the bank of the Weser. And Böttcherstrasse with its curved brick facades is home to both old merchant offices and chic new shops. Germany's smallest federal state harmoniously links past and present.

Bremen Town Musicians ▲

▼ Böttcherstraße

▼ Roland

Dozens of grey seals, Germany's largest predators, lounge on the sand dune immediately in front of the "red island". Seagulls, terns and guillemots make a racket in the precipitous rocks, while a keen wind whistles over the green plateau, tousling the sheep. Tall Anna, the symbol of Germany's sole ocean island, is still standing, although over time the sandstone has been deeply eroded by the sea and the storms.

▲ Tall Anna

▼ "Guillemots' Rock"

▼ Transfer by boat

Free and Hanseatic City of Hamburg

▲ Port with "Michel"

Hamburg is Germany's gateway to the world, bustling, international, elegant yet rich in romance. The new HafenCity dockland district, the magnificent neo-Renaissance town hall and the beautiful brick buildings from the 1920s like Chilehaus give the maritime metropolis on the Elbe a unique atmosphere. Shops of top designers from all over the world cluster around Jungfernstieg, while a faint aroma of cinnamon, cardamom and coffee still lingers in the brick ravines of the Speicherstadt warehouse district. Musicals and elegant shopping arcades like the Hanseviertel attract thousands of visitors, as does the Alsterarkaden arcade, which on sunny days recalls Venice. New attractions appear nearly every year. Recent highlights include the BallinStadt Emigrant Museum and Miniatur Wunderland, the world's largest model railway. Not to mention Hagenbeck Zoo, the trendy Schanzenviertel,

▲ Speicherstadt warehouse district

St. Pauli Landungsbrücken ▶

the fish market on Sundays – and, of course, St. Pauli. The "Kiez", the infamous red light district around the legendary Davidswache police station, has long since also become a venue for musicals, restaurants and night clubs.

The heart of Hamburg, however, remains its port. When a containership stacked with boxes as high as a multi-storey building comes in, or one of the departing white cruise liners sounds its horn, it's easy to get that romantic feeling "Junge-komm-bald-wieder" ("Come back again soon, lad" – Freddy Quinn's song).

▲ Binnenalster

▲ Town hall and arcades

▲ St. Pauli, Große Freiheit

North Frisia – islands and Halligwelt (world of small islands)

▲ St. Peter-Ording

▲ Hallig Südfall "land submerged"

Sylt, elbow ▶

▼ Island of Sylt

The rich and beautiful still savour Sylt. Seeing and being seen is the favourite sport in the "St. Tropez of the North". However, the VIPs have long since shared the island with the less affluent. Amrum with its heath and pine wood and the environment-conscious Föhr with its pretty Frisian villages are also totally tuned to tourists. Throughout Husum there is still something of the spirit of the "Schimmelreiter" ("The Ghost Rider"), the novella in which Theodor Storm immortalised the "grey town by the sea". And in Seebüll the Nolde Museum recalls the artist and his incomparable paintings of the expanse of sky over the flat land.

▲ Holtenau Locks

Shipping sets the scene. In Schleswig-Holstein's modern capital, shipbuilding and ferry services to Scandinavia play an important role. The big ships pass through the Holtenau Locks to transit the Kiel Canal. Kieler Woche is regarded as the world's largest sailing regatta.

The Navy Memorial inaugurated in Laboe in 1936 commemorates all fallen naval personnel. On clear days, you can see as far as Denmark from the top of the monument with its 341 steps. If you want to find out more about how the Port of Kiel originated and the work there, you will find all you need to know in the Shipping Museum.

▲ Laboe, U 995 and Navy Memorial

▲ Ferries in port

▲ Town hall and opera house

▲ Ferry

▲ Fehmarnsund Bridge

The Baltic is a gentle sea: somewhat less salty, less stormy, less raw than its impetuous sister, the North Sea. The Baltic has a very varied coastline with a succession of wide sandy beaches, tranquil bays and picturesque steep banks, constantly nibbled at by the restless sea. In spring, rape colours the land deep yellow, seagulls squawk and white clouds drift across the deep blue sky. In the harbours, fishing cutters sell plaice and cod freshly caught on board and the sails of the boats flap in the wind.

▲ Schleimünde Lighthouse ▼ Sailing ships off Travemünde

Steep banks ▶

The Baltic – roofed wicker beach chairs and sand castles

Only a few weeks later, it's high season in Grömitz, Scharbeutz and Timmendorf Beach. Sun worshippers of all ages lie in the hot sand, the ice-cream parlours are packed out and in the evening it's party time until the wee hours of the morning. There's a restless riviera feeling in the Bay of Lübeck, but it's somewhat more relaxed around Hohwacht. Peace then returns in autumn, when mists rise from the meadows on the Schlei, geese fly over the sun island of Fehmarn to the south, and kale and grog soon reappear on the menus.

▲ Darß

▼ Pier at dusk

Hanseatic City of Lübeck

Lübeck has a good reputation. This is where Thomas Mann and Willy Brandt were born; Lübeck marzipan is well-known all over the world, and for decades the famous Holstentor adorned the German 50-mark note. In the Middle Ages, the city with the seven spires was dubbed "Queen of the Hanseatic League". The great past is still recalled by the Holy Ghost

▼ Holstentor with St. Marien and St. Petri

▲Town hall

Hospital, cathedral and town hall with its various buildings from the 13th to the 16th c. The Gothic Marienkirche became the model for brick buildings throughout the Baltic region. New life has returned to the alleyways with their small craftsman dwellings in the backyards, and in the historic Schiffergesellschaft restaurant guests sit shoulder to shoulder at the meticulously scrubbed oak trestle tables and sip "Lübecker Rotspon", a delicious red wine. Lübeck is a lively picture-book in brick – and the sea is not far away. The ferries from Scandinavia berth in Travemünde, "Lübeck's beautiful daughter". Top hotels await their guests. And the four-masted barque "Passat" rocks in the wind.

▼ Baltic spa Travemünde

Buddenbrookhaus ▶

Mecklenburg-West Pomerania – brick Gothic and lots of lakes

▲ Stralsund

▲ Wismar

▲ Schwerin Palace
▼ Mecklenburg Lake District

Where ospreys circle, unique avenues lead like green tunnels through the countryside and old towns reflect an eventful history on their brick faces. That is Mecklenburg-West Pomerania. Curators of monuments and restorers have achieved a great deal in this region following the reunification of Germany. Numerous ramshackle historic buildings in danger of collapsing have been restored to new splendour. Thousands of visitors flock to marvel at the stone witnesses of the past, such as Schwerin Palace with its estimated 365 turrets, Wismar with its six monumental brick churches and Stralsund with its magnificent row of historic facades on the old market square. And far away in the depths of the countryside, nature's heritage has also been preserved: on the Schaalsee lake and on the river Müritz kayakers silently glide through the water, anglers hope to catch the pike of their life, and a bittern dully announces itself from the reeds.

Hanseatic City of Rostock and Baltic spa Warnemünde

▲ View over the Warnow to Rostock

Rostock, the largest city in Mecklenburg-West Pomerania, is known for its handsome churches and the beautiful, highly variegated facades of Kröpeliner Strasse. Hanse-Sail, during which windjammers from all over the world tie up in the port, attracts a million visitors annually. In Warnemünde, Rostock's summer resort, there's a smell of freshly smoked herring, ships honk all over the place, and from a hundred-year-old lighthouse you can follow the route of the ferries (almost) to Denmark.

▼ University

▼ Warnemünde, lighthouse

Baltic island Rügen, Hiddensee and Usedom

▼ Hiddensee, Dornbusch Lighthouse

▲ Chalky cliffs, Rügen

Rügen is known for its dramatic and varied landscape. The wild romanticism of the steep white cliffs of the Königsstuhl was superbly captured in paint by Caspar David Friedrich. Oh, the lonely forests, storm-tossed coasts, moors on which bees buzz and dragonflies whirr!

And then there's the sheer elegance of the island's sea-bathing business. Little palaces gleam; the white filigree spa architecture is superb. Villas have been transformed into charming hotels. Fashionable piers attract strollers, and between them historic train Rasender Roland, a bit of nostalgia on wheels, puffs between Putbus and Göhren.

▼ Rügen, Binz spa centre

Ahlbeck pier, Usedom ▲

On the lake Hiddensee you can then discover the fragrant heath and bird protection area, in which cranes, geese and terns rest and breed. The Danish silent film star Asta Nielsen had a house, the "Karusel", built here. Gerhard Hauptmann, author of "The Weavers", was buried on Rügen at his own request. In the Bodden waters of Usedom, perch and zander go thrashing into the fishermen's nets. The 40 km long beach has long since again become "Berlin's bathtub". Thatched houses, post windmills and reed-fringed lakes give the hinterland its special character. And the spa tradition lives triumphantly on at the "three sisters" of Bansin, Heringsdorf and Ahlbeck.

▲ Heringsdorf pier, Usedom

▼ Spa architecture

Berlin, Germany's capital

Victory Column

Who hasn't marched through here since the inauguration in 1791! The Prussian kings and Napoleon passed through Brandenburger Tor, the revolutionaries of 1848 and the Communists around Karl Liebknecht. In 1933, the Nazis announced their rule of terror by staging pompous marches, and after the second world war East and West, communism and capitalism, irreconcilably confronted one another at this "interface".

▼ Kaiser Wilhelm Memorial Church

▼ Charlottenburg Palace

◀ Brandenburg gate ▲ Reichstag ▼ Reichstag dome

Again and again, Brandenburger Tor has been a focal point of German history.
From 1961, the Wall – 155 km long, 4 metres high – divided the city. A little of it has remained. Two city centres developed over the years, and they can still be clearly made out: in the east, the district around Berlin-Mitte, and in the west, the area around Kürfürstendamm and Kaiser Wilhelm Memorial Church. The ruin of this church, which was bombed in the second world, was retained as a memorial. The modern Europa-Center was built opposite it in the early 1960s. The Department Store of the West, or "KaDeWe" for short, is the highlight at Wittenbergplatz. Anyone going up to the top floors will find their mouth watering at the sight of salami from the Abruzzo, French country bread, cheese from Brandenburger Höfe, Norwegian cod – the food department not only fulfils all wishes but also whets the appetite for new delights.
In November 1989, when the Wall was opened, East Berliners flocked through Brandenburger Tor in the direction of the Zoo station, while curious Charlottenburgers set off to take a look at Prenzlauer Berg. Germany was to grow together again, with Berlin as its new capital setting an example. The Reichstag became the symbol of unity. The sedate building was given an impressive glass dome by the British architect Sir Norman Foster. At the nearby Potsdamer Platz, Daimler, Sony, Deutsche Bahn, etc. moved into office towers glittering with glass and chrome alongside shopping paradises with colourful neon lights. Architects such as Helmut Jahn, Renzo Piano and Hans Kollhoff could realise visions. Cinemas, discos, a casino, five-star hotels and select shopping arcades crowd together today in a confined space – 2,600t of steel and glass formed into unusual shapes.

▲ Sony Center

▲ Checkpoint Charlie

Museum Island ▶

What a lot there is to do here! A visit to what is probably Berlin's most beautiful square, Gendarmenmarkt with its two cathedrals, is a "must". Checkpoint Charlie recalls the division of the city. The Museum Island features the famous Pergamon Altar and a bust of Nofretete. A boat trip through the canals reveals a totally unknown Berlin from the water.

▼ Gendarmenmarkt

Looking down from the top of the TV tower, you have the entire metropolis at your feet 200 metres below. The Staatsoper and Schauspielhaus on the famous boulevard Unter den Linden put on attractive performances. The splendidly restored Hackesche Höfe with Jugendstil facades promise happy shopping, and in the adventurous cultural centre Tacheles you'll still perhaps have a chance of experiencing an exciting performance by a budding world star for a reasonable price. There is a wealth of international flair in Kreuzberg and Prenzlauer Berg: the pubs, clubs, bio markets, trendy clothes shops and art cinemas are very popular, the only problem being that among all the Swabians, Turks, Franconians, Serbs and Münsterländers you very seldom come across that rare species: genuine Berliners!

▲ National Gallery ▼ Berlin Cathedral

Potsdam – former seat of the Prussian court

▲ Glienicke Bridge

▲ Cecilienhof Palace

Potsdam is an almost inconceivably beautiful townscape. And it's not only Sanssouci, the palace built by the architect Knobelsdorff for Frederick II, a long building with a yellow rococo facade overlooking green terraces, that

▼ Sanssouci, Chinese Tea House

◀"Old Fritz", Frederick II ▼ Sanssouci Palace

▲ Alter Markt with Nikolaikirche

▲ Nauener Gate and Dutch quarter

delights visitors. Other attractions are the ornate Chinese Tea House in the park, the 240m long, pink and white New Palace with its marble gallery, the Roman Baths (1835), an orangery showing Italian influence and an historic mill, all forming an elegant and ornate ensemble. And in the town itself old gates and a royal stables, today a film museum, recall the old Prussia, when the "long fellows", the tall soldiers of Old Fritz, paraded through the streets.

▲ Marble Palace, New Garden

▲ Altes Land ▼ Gabled houses in Lüneburg

Between Altes Land and Weserbergland

In spring, Altes Land still sinks into a sea of cherry and apple blossoms. Shepherds wander with their flocks through the heath. And the Pied Piper of Hamelin still heads a swarm of yelling children. The medieval facades in the Hanseatic City of Lüneburg bear witness to its former wealth, based on the salt trade, while the ducal palace in Celle, seat of a court, has been a resplendent baroque edifice since the 17th c. However, today the Car Museum in Wolfsburg presents just as fascinating a show about the world-famous Volkswagen "Käfer", or "Beetle". In Minden, the Mittellandkanal crosses the Weser on a 370m long bridge – a technical masterpiece. And traditional Bad Pyrmont with its modern therapy centres and sauna landscapes has become one of Germany's three most attractive spa locations.

◀ Celle Stallion Parade ▼ Celle Palace

▲ Wolfsburg ▼ Heidschnucke sheep on Lüneburg Heath ▲ Minden/Weser, Mittellandkanal ▼ Hamelin

▼ Bad Pyrmont

State capital Hanover

▲ Trade fair

▲ Herrenhausen Gardens

Hanover Fair has made the city world-famous. The metropolis of Lower Saxony is always at the frontfront when it comes to capital goods, computers or home textiles. Yet these are not the only highlights: the Herrenhausen Gardens are among the most beautiful baroque gardens in Germany, the Expo Zoo is one of the most up-to-date of its kind, and for purity of architectural style the town hall can hardly be matched: almost all of it looks as if it dated from the 15th c.

▲ Nana ▼ Town hall

▲ Brunswick, Burgplatz

The walls of both these towns breathe history. Brunswick was the seat of Henry the Lion. Dankwarderode Castle and the Column of the Lion still recall the ruler who was Duke of Bavaria and Saxony and is buried in the cathedral of St. Blasius. Hildesheim has had its own bishop since 815. The Knochenhaueramtshaus is regarded as the "most beautiful half-timbered house in the world". The church of St. Michael and the cathedral belong to the UNESCO world cultural heritage, and the adjoining rose bush deserves the same privilege, as it is said to have been in bloom for at least a thousand years.

▼ Hildesheim, Knochenhaueramtshaus

▼ Hildesheim, St. Michaelis

The Harz – mountain landscape steeped in legends

▲ Goslar, Kaiserpfalz

▲ Harzquerbahn railway network

It's a truly legendary landscape! And no wonder: when the fog wreathes the Brocken mountain in grey clouds and the storm howls in the spruces, it's easy to imagine the witches flying in on their broomsticks on Walpurgis Night to confer and plot their next move.

But this area is known far more for its flesh-and-blood celebrities. Martin Luther, for instance, who is recalled by a museum in Eisleben, was born here. German emperors built their largest palatinate complex in Goslar, the "Northern Rome", in the 11th c.

▲ Wernigerode, town hall

▼ Rammelsberg Mining Museum

▼ Okerstausee

◀ Brocken

▲ Quedlinburg, Schlossberg

▲ Rosstrappe

▼ Hahnenklee

Close by, in Rammelsberg, men may have dug for ore 3,000 years ago. In Wernigerode, the locals built a "gambling house" in Lower Saxon half-timbered style in the 16th c. – and shortly afterwards converted it into their town hall, one of the most beautiful in Europe. In Quedlinburg, where 1,200 half-timbered houses are now waiting to be successively renovated, Heinrich I lies buried in Servatius church. And the magnificent cathedral treasure glitters and gleams under glass.

Between Teutoburg Forest and Weserbergland

▲ Extern Stones

▲ Porta Westfalica

▼ Corvey Palace

The Weser breaks violently through at Porta Westfalica into the lowland between the Wiehen and Weser Mountains. The land is known for its moors, lush meadows, wide, barren plateaus – and over 100 mills. The spiritual centre of Europe was located here in the Middle Ages: Corvey Monastery, founded in 822 in Höxter, attracted thinkers and mystics from all over. This is also where the Brothers Grimm collected their fairy tales, which still live today along the“ German Fairytale Route”.

▼ Shipping on the Weser near Höxter

▲ Hann. Münden, town hall

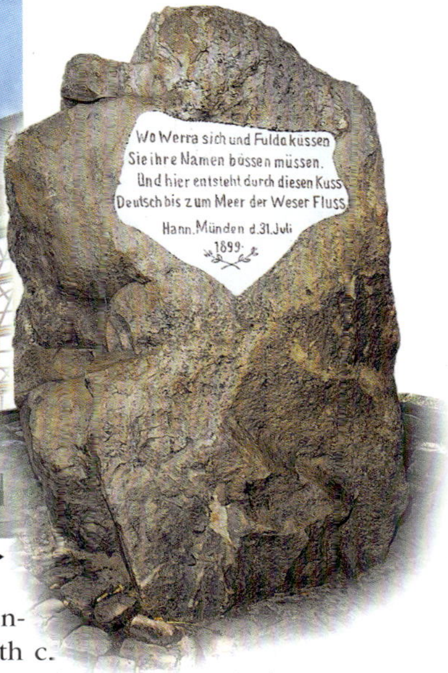

Weser Stone ▶

The region along the Weser is home to legends and great storytellers. In Hessisch Oldendorf, the locals lived in dread of the evil Baxmann, who simply did not want to die. Wilhelm Busch was born in Wiedensahl. Doctor Eisenbart, reputed to have wicked treatment methods (even though he was in reality a very successful, modern doctor) worked in Hannoversch Münden in the 17th c. And Göttingen is famous not only for its university of 1734, which produced 40 Nobel prize winners – the Gänseliesel on the market square is the most kissed girl in the world: all those who have just acquired a doctorate imprint a "little one" on her.

▼ Göttingen, Gänseliesel Fountain

▼ Göttingen, town hall

Münsterland – moated castles and cyclists' paradise

▲ Vischering Castle

Anholt Palace ▶

▲ Münster, palace

▲ Münster, town hall

▼ Cycle city Münster

Palaces mirrored in the water, magnificent manor houses, well-fortified castles with drawbridge and embrasures – over 100 such buildings still stand guard, stone witnesses of a lordly past, in Münsterland. And scattered in between you find gardens: farmers' gardens, botanical gardens, baroque gardens, school gardens, ultra-modern garden landscapes – Münsterland is garden land. And Münster is right in the middle of it all. Münster with its Prinzipalmarkt arcades, the impressive St. Paulus Cathedral and the iron cages on Lamberti church, where in 1536 the corpses of the Anabaptists were paraded after they had been tortured and stabbed to death. The Peace of Westphalia ending the Thirty Years' War was concluded in Münster in 1648. The Kiepenkerl monument recalls the itinerant dealers of yore who brought baskets of eggs, chickens and milk from the surrounding countryside to the house doors. Today, Münster has many faces: it is, for instance, the cyclists' capital, a cultural hub, the favourite destination of thousands of students and the location of the popular All Weather Zoo.

Kiepenkerl ▶

▲ Krefeld, Linn Castle

This is a beautiful region, as the Romans also discovered. They founded a military camp here in the 1st c. BC. From here, the later Xanten, General Varus led his legions against Armin the Cheruscan in 9 AD – and suffered a devastating defeat. But history went on, leaving behind many other traces in the area: the tower Schwanenturm of Kleve, the state castle of the Electorate of Cologne in Kempen, the German Textile Museum in Krefeld. The lighter side of life is represented by the Academy of Fools in Viersen, on the Rhine promenade at Rees and on Germany's longest suspension bridge in Emmerich. Then there is plenty of piety in Kevelaer: pilgrims have flocked to St. Maria since 1642. Hundreds of thousands still come every year. What's more, since 1985 many have also arrived on their motorbikes.

▲ Kevelaer, place of pilgrimage

◀ Xanten, Roman town

▲ Lower Rhine

▲ Essen, Zollverein mining complex

▲ Essen, "Stille Lagerung"

▲ Essen, Villa Hügel

▼ Duisburg, Landschaftspark Nord

▲ Schalke fans

▲ Carnival

The sky used to be grey above the Ruhr, and the red dust that spewed out of the smokestacks lay thick on the window seats. But that was quite a long time ago. Mines have become museums, steelworks leisure parks and monuments. Gasometer Oberhausen is now used as an exhibition hall, while the old mine in Essen has been designated part of the UNESCO world cultural heritage. The most outstanding examples of converted plants are on the "Route of Industrial Culture". Industrialisation admittedly hasn't completely died out: the Port of Duisburg is still regarded as the world's foremost inland port. But, generally speaking, there is a lot of green to be seen in the "Revier", one of the largest conurbations in Europe, with a wealth of landscape parks and nature reserves. Bochum, Recklinghausen, Essen and Oberhausen are cultural centres with highly regarded opera houses, art museums, theatres and musical theatres. And, of course, football is at home here. Hearts still beat ever faster in Dortmund and Gelsenkirchen on Saturday afternoons at three o clock when the whistle blows for a football match. Hey lads! It's a Federal League match!

▼ Solingen

Wuppertal, suspension railway ▼

Rhine metropolis and cathedral city of Cologne

Naturally, as the folk song puts it, we'll leave the "Dom zu Kölle" (the cathedral in Cologne) – where otherwise would it tower so majestically over the sea of houses and be reflected in such a golden light in the Rhine? The foundation stone was laid in 1248, at a time when Cologne was the third richest city in Europe. However, it took exactly 632 years until the last stone was fitted into place in 1880 and this masterpiece of Gothic with its 157m high towers was finally completed. The twelve Romanesque churches of Cologne, all built between the 11th and the 13th c., are even older and no less important. The Roman-Germanic Museum, which was erected over the famous Dionysos Mosaic from the 2nd c. AD and brings the time of the founding of the town to life, goes even further back in history. There are countless pictures in the museums: art from the Middle Ages up to the 19th c. in the Wallraff Richartz Museum and modern works of the 20th c. in Museum Ludwig.

So much for the serious side. Right – but Cologne is just as much the city of mirth. Its carnival is world-famous. The Shrove Monday procession is legendary. That's when everyone says "Alaaf!" ("Hullo!") as greeting. And Kölsch is popular among both the locals and the visitors: it's the genuine, light, top-fermented Cologne beer.

▼ Gross St. Martin

▼ St. Pantaleon

▼ Cathedral "Lamentation of Christ"

▼ Cathedral, portal

State capital Düsseldorf

Art is at home here, along with fashion, constantly coming up with new ideas – and there are vast numbers of Japanese managers. The capital of North Rhine-Westphalia is at one and the same time transport hub, administrative centre and major industrial location. Joseph Beuys breathed new life into the Art Academy. Fashion schools develop trends that are premiered at the trade fairs today and will already be found tomorrow in the boutiques of Königsallee. And at the "longest bar in the world", comprising over 250 bars and restaurants in the old town, models, painters and managers get together over a good dark beer.

▼ Rhine bank with castle tower ▲ Rhine tower

▶ "Kö"

◀ Media Port

▲ Postwagen

▲ Town hall

This is where German kings were crowned and the remains of Charlemagne rest in a golden shrine. Aachen Cathedral is major monument and has truly magnificent treasures. Over 100 ecclesiastical works of art from late antiquity to Gothic – from the Lothar cross set with precious stones to the silver-golden bust of Charlemagne to the relief-adorned vessel of ivory – shimmer and gleam in the cases beneath the octagonal domed building.

▲ Cathedral Treasury

▼ Aachen Cathedral

Wonderful Hesse

▲ Limburg on the Lahn

▲ German Limesstrasse, Roman castle Saarburg

There's money in Frankfurt. But the government is in Wiesbaden. This distinguished capital with its elegant casino, spa centre and state theatre still has the splendour of the golden age of the spas. But other towns in the federal state of Hesse can also certainly hold their own. Marburg defends its reputation as seat of a liberal university. Limburg is known for its seven-towered cathedral, a blend of Romanesque and early Gothic.

▲ University town Marburg ▼ Taunus, Königstein Fortress ▼ Darmstadt, Mathildenhöhe ▲ Wiesbaden, spa centre

▲ Rhone, water peak

▲ Fulda, cathedral

▼ Rhone, Mount Calvary

Darmstadt's attractions are the Wedding Tower and the Mathildenhöhe artists' quarter, where Jugendstil was once triumphant. Venerable Fulda on the river Fulda, old heart of the Frankish empire, was founded as early as 744 by St. Boniface, whose remains lie today in the crypt of the baroque cathedral. In the Peasants' Wars, 10,000 oppressed farmers in the Fulda countryside rose up against the authorities. During the witch trials in the 17th c., 300 citizens were allegedly tortured and burnt to death.

So much history, so much culture – and nature, too, is always very present. The forests of the Taunus, for instance, where the busy people of Frankfurt seek rest and relaxation at the weekend. The Rhone, the centre of Germany, offers visitors an impressive 6,000 km of foot-paths. Black-headed Rhone sheep roam over the moors and windy plateaus, which have been a UNESCO biosphere reservation since 1991. Since the early 20th century, gliders have taken off from the 950m high water peak. And the bronze eagle keeps a watchful eye on everything that's going on.

Kassel – city of art and culture

Every four years, Kassel becomes an international metropolis. At "documenta", artists from all over the world show us where art currently is in pictures, objects and installations. These exhibitions leave behind lasting traces: Joseph Beuys' 7,000 oaks, for instance. Thomas Schütte's larger than life-size terracotta figures. Claes Oldenburg's blue pick. Or Jonathan Borowsky's "Skywalker". All this is embedded in the wonderful Karlsaue Park from the age of baroque.

▲ Fridericianum

▲ Orangery

Admire the rococo garden of Wilhelmsthal Palace. And Wilhelmshöhe, Europe's largest mountain park with its over 8m high Hercules. The fountain display at his feet delights onlookers in summer: 1,200 m³ of water gushes down over cascades, a waterfall, the devil bridge and an aqueduct for an hour and finally shoots up as a fountain 25m up into the sky in the palace pond.

◀ Bad Wilhelmshöhe

▲ Skywalker

▲ Skyline

The city is known for its stock exchange and banks, of course, and its shiny office towers studding the skyline. The Römer, the venerable town hall for 600 years, in which kings and emperors were crowned. The Paulskirche of red sandstone, where the National Meeting, the first entire German parliament, convened in 1848. Palm garden, zoo and museum bank. The old opera house, which was bombed in 1944 and splendidly restored and reopened in 1981. Not to mention the Schirn-Kunsthalle, which presents exciting avantgarde art. The Fressgass, where you can savour the local sausages, "Handkäs" cheese and green sauce. And, of course, the city's greatest son – born in Goethehaus, honoured in the Goethe Museum. But now it's off to Sachsenhausen: it's Ebbelwoi-Zeit (cider time)! A cider please, waitress!

▼ "Bull and bear" in front of the stock exchange

Römer ▶ town hall

Saxony-Anhalt – a state steeped in German history

▲ Tangermünde on the Elbe

▲ Stendal, Uenglinger Tor

▼ Stendal, Roland

There is a long list of famous names hailing from the state between Harz and Elbe. In Wittenberg, Martin Luther nailed his 95 theses on the church door, thereby bringing about an historical upheaval. Handel, the composer of the "Water Music", was born in Halle, which was also the birthplace of the painter Lyonel Feininger and the former German foreign minister Hans-Dietrich Genscher. In Mansfeld, the poet Novalis searched for the blue flower of Romanticism. Bismarck is a son of the Altmark. The philosopher Nietzsche was born in Röcken near Lützen and is buried there.

▼ Dessau, Bauhaus

▼ Garden Kingdom of Dessau-Wörlitz

▲ Luther town Wittenberg

Luther town Wittenberg, Theses Door ▶

The various epochs have left a legacy of a wide range of styles and buildings. There are the mighty castles of Querfurt and of Neuenburg, which stands guard over the Saale-Unstrut valley, home of a very fine wine. There are over 70 churches, gates and facades with the typical round arches on the "Romanesque Road". A city like Halle has buildings from Gothic times up to the present day – including a large number of the typical GDR prefabricated buildings. Finally, the North German brick buildings in Stendal and Tangermünde must also be included on the list. Not to mention the Bauhaus in Dessau, which in the early 20th c. inspired the simplicity and clear lines of modern classic design.

The land has plenty of green countryside and is richly endowed with rivers, gardens and parks. The most beautiful of all is undoubtedly the Garden Kingdom of Dessau-Wörlitz: 112 ha of park landscape, created along English lines, lavishly adorned with bridges, canals, tea houses, pagodas and an orangery – a green baroque marvel.

◀ Handel

Halle on the Saale, market square ▶

State capital Magdeburg

▲ View over the Elbe to cathedral

▲ Town hall with Magdeburg Rider

▼ Magdalenenkapelle chapel and St. Petri

The artist Hundertwasser set his "Green Citadel" cheekily between the Gothic cathedral, the austere monastery Unser Lieben Frauen and the Magdeburg Rider, who has throned over the old market since the mid-13th c. The late Austrian artist also wanted the residential and commercial buildings in the citadel, completed in 2005, to be an "oasis for humanity and nature". A playful round, pink dab of colour, the citadel forms an unusual, gleaming gold contrast to the severe lines of the many classic buildings in the state capital.

Hundertwasser's green citadel ▶

▲ Pücklerpark Branitz

Spree Forest cultural landscape and biosphere reservation

▲ In the Spree Forest ▼ Spree Forest historic costume

A very individual and appealing part of Germany has kept its identity in remote southern Brandenburg, where the postman still sometimes comes by barge, the cucumbers seasoned with spice, pepper, garlic or mustard are crunchy, and the Sorbs, who have made their home here since 6th c., put on their attractive traditional costume for all important events and paint Easter eggs with the age-old designs. And for canoeists, campers, anglers and all those who want to escape the din of the urban world this network of meandering waterways stretching for hundreds of kilometres is, in any case, a true paradise.

▼ Trip by skiff in the Spree Forest

▲ China town Meissen   Moritzburg Hunting Castle ▶

Saxony was rich, as its many palaces, castles and parks still reveal. In the past, anyone who thought he was somebody and had well-filled coffers had one of the magnificent buildings erected – on a basalt cone, like Königstein Fortress, in the Mulde valley, such as Colditz Castle from the Renaissance, or idyllically located in the midst of ponds, like Moritzburg Hunting Palace, with its collection of antlers and the Feather Room displaying millions of different birds' feathers. The owners of these splendid edifices put on sumptuous festivals, employed court composers and dined off "white gold", Meissen china – only the genuine article with the crossed swords. The ordinary people meanwhile created their own culture: in the Ore Mountains, they carved smoking men and nutcrackers; in Vogtland, the locals made violins and filigree lace. In the Ore Mountains, the miners marched in uniform through the towns, lustily singing the miners'

▼ Ore Mountains, miners'parade in Freiberg

▼ Zittauer Mountains, Qybin

song "Glück auf, der Steiger kommt" ("Good luck, the miner's coming").
And all this has been kept alive for visitors today. And perhaps they also hear, while lingering over a fine wine from the Saxon Wine Route, one of the old legends that are still alive in the land. The one about the Maiden's Leap from Qybin, for instance, concerning a pious young woman, who, pursued by a lecherous monk, is said in her desperation to have jumped from the rock, 50m down to certain death. But, miraculously, her skirt opened wide, and she floated gently down, like a parachute, into the valley. But the monk roared with anger, leapt into the abyss and was never seen again. That was the devil, no doubt about it.

▲ Görlitz

▼ Bautzen

▼ Vogtland, Embroidery Presentation Plauen

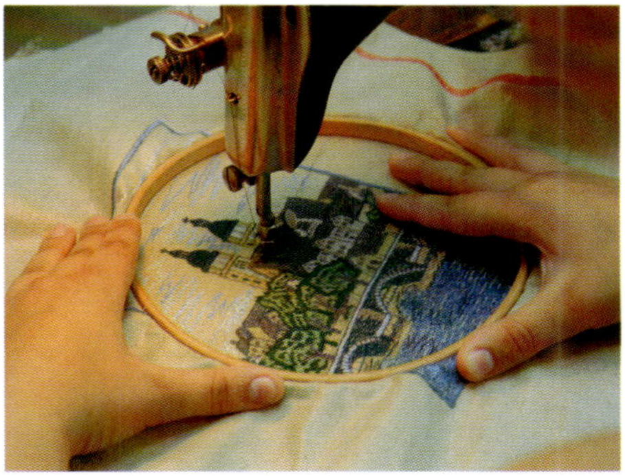

▼ Vogtland, Göltzsch Valley Bridge

Dresden – former seat of the Saxon court

Is it "the most beautiful town in Germany", as its inhabitants claim? That might well be. At all events, the collection of buildings that the Saxon kings had built for themselves in the course of a few centuries is unique. Dresden is a beautiful baroque ensemble.

The Frauenkirche, which was reopened in 2005 after a ten-year renovation, dominates the entire panorama. The Semper Opera House on Theaterplatz is reminiscent of an attractive Italian country house. The Zwinger was modelled on the Versailles orangery, creating a magnificent playground for royal festivities. Today it accommodates art galleries of the old (Rubens, Raffael, Rembrandt) and new masters (Otto Dix, Max Liebermann and Max Slevogt). The

▲ Zwinger

▼ Semper Opera House

Golden Rider ▲

Fürstenzug (Princely Procession) presents the history of the Princely House of Wettin on 25,000 Meissen china tiles and was re-enacted with real horses and riders for the 800th anniversary celebration of the city in 2006. And on Hauptstrasse in Neustadt August the Strong gleams and glitters on his high horse as the Golden Rider. The gold-plated copper statue was set up in the early 18th c.

▼ Fürstenzug (Princely Procession)

▲▼ Frauenkirche

Elbe Sandstone Mountains – unique hiking and natural paradise

"Wildly romantic" – seldom does a term describe a region more aptly. Down through the millennia, rain and wind have etched deep ravines into the sandstone, sculpting individual pillars and creating adventurous-looking, deeply forested gorges. The about 76m stone Bastei bridge spans the abyss. The Elbe Sandstone Mountains in the heart of Saxon Switzerland is a real paradise for climbers and an ideal landscape for romantics – the painter Caspar David Friedrich frequently derived inspiration from the stone teeth. From the lookout point of the Bastei, we look down on the Elbe, along which pass the ships of the White Fleet. In summer, Winnetou and his white blood brother Old Shatterhand shake hands on the rock stage of Rathen. In the background rises Königstein Fortress, in which August the Strong had the alchemist Johann Friedrich Böttger incarcerated. He was instructed to invent artificial gold to fill the ever empty state coffers. Nothing came of it. Instead, the involuntary scientist discovered another exquisite treasure: china. In 1710, the Elector established the first factory for "white gold" in Meissen.

▲ Königstein fortress

▼ View from the Bastei

▼ Bastei bridge

Trade fair and university city Leipzig

“Little Paris”, “Mother of all fairs”, “Bach city”, “Boomtown of the east” – Leipzig has many honorary titles with which to adorn itself. The city is expanding – yet retaining its traditional core. The main station (1915) has been given a completely new “inner life” with nearly 150 shops. Auerbach’s Cellar, featured in Goethe’s “Faust”, is located between international brand boutiques in the Mädlerpassage arcade. In the old cotton spinning mill, once the largest in Europe, architects, designers, artists and fashion makers now create the future. The world-famous Thomanerchor still sings in the Thomaskirche, while in the Gewandhaus the no less famous Gewandhaus orchestra holds its concerts – and outside new glass and aluminium facades go up day by day. Leipzig is an alert place: the big Monday demonstrations protesting against the East German government started in 1989 from the prayers for peace in Nikolaikirche.

▲ Thomaskirche ▼ Main station

▲ Augustusplatz

Old town hall ▶

Thuringia, free state in the heart of Germany

▲ Kyffhäuser

Eisenach, Wartburg ▶

▲ Erfurt, cathedral and Severikirche

"Oh, I so like wandering on the Rennsteig through the land, knapsack on my back, guitar in my hand ..." – that's how it begins, the hymn of Germany's most famous foot-path. The 168.3 km long Rennsteig passes through the Thuringinian Forest, under pines, firs and beeches, over green tops and gently undulating hills, past Grosser Inselsberg, also called "King of the Thuringian Forest" on account of its magnificent view. However, Thuringia is not only one of the greenest regions in Germany but also rich in history. Business, culture and religion are deeply rooted here. In Jena, Carl Zeiss developed his fine optical glasses, creating a brand with a worldwide reputation. In Erfurt,

▼ Jena, Zeiss-Planetarium

Eisenach ▶

the state capital, there are about 20 old churches and monasteries. Friedenstein Palace in Gotha was the first baroque palace in Germany and has a theatre with technology from the 18th c. that still works! In Schmalkalden, the Protestant estates fought against the Catholic emperor. And the Wartburg towers over everything, with its own place in German history: in 1206, the most prominent Minnesänger (troubadours) allegedly met here for the famous "Sängerkrieg" – today hip-hoppers have revived the tradition. Here, too, St. Elisabeth distributed her alms and Martin Luther translated the New Testament.

This is also where 500 students met for the Wartburgfest in 1817 and demanded "Honour – Freedom – Fatherland": the divided Empire was finally to unite.

▲ Grosser Inselsberg

▲ Gotha, Friedenstein Palace

◀ Schmalkalden

▼ Trusetal Waterfall

Weimar – European cultural centre

▲ Belvedere Palace

▲ Goethe's house

▲ Duchess Anna Amalia Library

As one might say rather disrespectfully, Weimar is the centre of the superstars of German literature. Traditionally, however, it is described rather as the "cradle of German classics". Whatever you call it, Weimar is where the really great lived and worked. Goethe was minister at the court of Duke Carl August, and Schiller settled in Weimar in 1799.

The National Theatre was the venue of another important milestone of German history. The "Weimar Republic" was founded there in 1919, but unfortunately lasted only until 1933. The notorious Buchenwald concentration camp, in which the National Socialists murdered over 50,000 prisoners, is also part of German and Weimar history.

The master of the German language is remembered everywhere in Weimar. In their summer-

◀ Schiller House

▼ Goethe's Summer House

▲ Town palace

Town hall ▶

houses, it seems as if Goethe and Schiller had only just left for a little stroll. The rooms of the Schillerhaus, in which the famous dramatist spent the last three years of his life, writing works including "Wilhelm Tell", have been restored to their original condition, and a museum added. However, Goethe and Schiller are not the only two great personalities who added lustre to Weimar. Herder and Wieland are further names – as well as Johann Sebastian Bach, Liszt and Nietzsche.

It was Duchess Anna-Amalia who originally promoted this rich cultural life. Unfortunately 50,000 irreplaceable volumes in her library were destroyed in a fire in the Green Palace in 2004.

The library, which has over 800,000 books, was renovated and reopened in 2007.

And if after a cultural diet of so many classics you ever crave a snack, there's no need to panic: there's a nice smell of sausages somewhere ... the famous Thüringer Bratwürste are sizzling on the grills all over town. Tuck into a roll with a dab of original Thuringian mustard – while Goethe and Schiller look understandingly down from their pedestals.

▼ National Theatre

Goethe and Schiller monument ▶

Castles on the Rhine

▲ Rheinstein Castle

Katz Castle and Loreley Rock ▶

"Up there the most gorgeously beautiful maiden is sitting; her golden jewellery sparkles and she is combing her golden hair," penned Heinrich Heine. No wonder that the boatmen on the river couldn't take their eyes off her, the current and dangerous shallows suddenly seeming so unimportant to them – and they kept on gazing until their boats smashed on one of the treacherous underwater rocks and went under, the seductive Loreley having once again lured more of her victims to their doom.

Why is it so beautiful on the Rhine? Yes, indeed, we may well ask. Because "Rhine" rhymes with "wine". Because the river flows so peacefully and majestically past, carrying along with it white excursion steamers and portly barges. Because in the mornings the church spires of the villages emerge out of the haze, while in the evenings the slopes are bathed in a golden light. And because castles greet us from every rock: there are 28 of them just between Rüdesheim and Koblenz, including some dating from the 14th c., like the impressive fortress of Marksburg above Braubach. And ruins, rebuilt in the 19th c. at a time of enthusiasm for the age of knightly chivalry. Rheinstein Castle, refur-

◀ Loreley

▼ Rolandsbogen

bished by an opera singer at the end of the 19th century, is an example. Or Katz Castle, which today accommodates a hotel. And when on quite a few summer days the Rhine is aflame with fountains of light shooting into the night sky, sheaves of stars shining down on the old walls and the thunder of saluting guns echoing in the river valley, the visitor stands silently, marvels – and suddenly knows exactly why it's so beautiful on the Rhine.

▼ Pfalzgrafenstein Castle

Marksburg ▶

The Mosel – romantic winegrowing region

▲ Koblenz, Deutsches Eck

▲ Wine harvest

Piesporter Michelsberg, Zellers Schwarze Katz, Kröver Nacktarsch, Bernkastler Kürfurstlay – those were the wines with which post-war Germany grew up. Sweet, delicious Mosel was the quintessence of a "fine wine". Even the Romans prized these wines when they settled on the Mosel – and also gladly traded them, as shown by the Neumagen wine ship loaded with barrels featured on the tombstone of a Roman wine dealer that was discovered in 1878 during excavation work. A wooden replica of this vessel has curved over the Mosel since 2007.

Riesling, Elbling and Müller-Thurgau grow to maturity on steep slate slopes – in Bremme even on a 380m high slope with an incline of 68°, Bremmer Calmont being the steepest vineyard in Europe. And among the vineyards winegrowers invite visitors to winetastings, vintners' taverns have opened, the Reichsburg

▼ Saarburg

Neumagen, Roman wine ship

▲ Bremmer Mosel bend

▼ Eltz Castle

◀ Bernkastel-Kues

in Cochem rears defiantly up above the river, and tourists flock to attractive spots like Bernkastel-Kues. This town with its 400 year-old half-timbered facades, venerable Renaissance town hall and Michaelsbrunnen fountain (1608) seems as idyllic as if it had just been put together out of a box of Middle Ages building blocks. The most charming building of them all is the Spitzhäuschen (1416), which is how wine-growers' houses used to look: small and narrow, with a projecting upper storey and a high pointed warehouse.
The Mosel flows into the Rhine at Koblenz. At Deutsches Eck, where for years a flag warned people not to forget the unity of Germany, the old Emperor Wilhelm I astride his horse now once again keeps watch to ensure everything is in order.

▼ Cochem, Reichsburg

Trier – oldest city in Germany

◀ "Holy Coat"

▲ Cathedral

16 BC is a record. With this "date of birth", its founding by Emperor Augustus, Trier cannot be beaten – no place in Germany is older. Trier was also a bishop's seat in the 3rd c. It has the oldest cathedral in Germany, St. Peter's, and the best preserved Roman city gate north of the Alps, Porta Nigra. The imperial thermal baths, Roman bridge and ruins of the amphitheatre are famous. As many as nine buildings in Trier belong to the UNESCO world cultural heritage. And let's not forget that Karl Marx was born in Trier in 1818.

◀ Electoral palace and basilica

▼ Porta Nigra

▲ Imperial thermal baths

▲ Die 3 Maare near Daun

Manderscheid castles ▶

The Eifel is a mosaic of extremely varied landscapes with high moors like the High Venn, ravines such as the Devil's Hole, rapids like the Irrel Waterfalls, volcanic fields, juniper heaths, basalt domes and, of course, the circular "Maare" lakes, left behind by the volcanoes. It's a paradise for hikers, climbers, swimmers and cyclists. The plateaus also provide excellent protection for the vineyard slopes of the Ahr.

The climate is thus extremely mild on the 89 km long tributary of the Rhine, the slopes storing the warmth and creating ideal conditions for red grapes. And that is precisely why the Ahr is so well-known as the largest red wine area in Germany.

▼ Vineyards in Ahrtal

The Saar – industrial heritage and French way of life

▲ Völklinger Hütte

▲ Saarbrücken

▲ Mettlacher Abbey ▼ Saar Bend at Mettlach

For a century, the hammers resounded in the steelworks – then it was all over. The lights in Völklingen Ironworks went out in 1986. In 1994, the steel jungle of pipes, lifts, overhead conveyors and blasting halls became the first industrial monument to be designated part of the UNESCO world cultural heritage. Today in the shadow of the six blast furnaces the rock band basses boom, films are made and the "Ferrodrom" shows a fascinating exhibition on the world of iron. But it's not only the laser beams of the light show that illuminate the night sky – some culinary stars also always sparkle more brightly here than elsewhere. France is close at hand, which is evident from the menu. Apart from "Gefillde" and "Hoorische" (filled and raw potato dumplings), guests can sample "Boudain" (blood sausage) and "Pommes dauphine" (Duchess potatoes). Bon appetit, everybody!

▲ Bad Kreuznach

▲ Idar-Oberstein

What a demonstration in the sunny Palatinate! On May 27th 1832, 30,000 people from many nations marched up to the ruin of Hambach Palace to demand freedom, civil rights, national unity and religious tolerance and ceremoniously unfurled a black-red-gold flag. The palace ruin was rebuilt 150 years later, and a new exhibition now recalls the significance of the festival.

The little Schweigen-Rechtenbach is regarded as "gateway" on the German Wine Route. Bad Dürkheim loves records. The largest wine barrel in the world would take 1.7 million litres, but is used as a restaurant. And the largest wine festival in the world is celebrated at the Dürkheim Sausage Market in September. Idar Oberstein is famous for its precious stone industry, the German Precious Stone Museum and a precious stone mine, which can be visited. Bad Kreuznach is a recognised mineral spa and has five rehabilitation clinics.

And what do they have in common, the towns and all the small villages in between, the cheerful people living on the banks of the Nahe? The love of wine, the southern way of life. A certain lightness of being.

▶ Schweigen-Rechtenbach
▶ Neustadt/Wine Route Hambach Palace
▼ Bad Dürkheim, giant barrel

Towns on the Rhine

▲ Rüdesheim, Drosselgassse

▲ Beethoven town Bonn

▲ Mainz, cathedral and Gutenberg monument

So much history is at home here: from Bonn, where Beethoven was born, the chancellors and ministers determined the fortunes of the Federal Republic for 50 years. In the cathedral city of Mainz, the Gutenberg Museum shows how the city's greatest son was responsible for one of mankind's most important inventions – and one of the few Bibles printed by him is on display as well. The songs of the tourists merry from wine have rung through the romantic alleys of Rüdesheim for decades – while the cash registers of the publicans ring out just as strongly. Finally, there is Worms, the city of the greatest heroic Germans sagas: here the noble Siegfried of Xanten wooed the king's daughter, here Kriemhild later quarrelled with Brunhilde over who was to enter the church first, here the malicious Hagen sank the treasure of the Nibelungs in the Rhine.

Whereupon, as everyone knows, the entire tragic history ended in an almighty bloodbath at the court of Etzel, king of the Huns. You can see it all every year at the Nibelung Festival.

Worms, Nibelungen bridge and cathedral ▶

▲ Speyer

▲ Lorsch Monastery

The Odenwald is the forest of the legends. The boulder field at Reichenbach, for instance, is said to have originated when two neighbouring giants quarrelled and pelted one another with boulders. The one from Feldberg was the weaker of the two and was buried by his opponent under a hail of stones, but sometimes you can still hear him roaring from the depths. The Michelstadt town hall (1484), one of the most beautiful half-timbered houses of the Middle Ages, also looks like a fairy-tale house. Speyer Cathedral is part of real history as the largest Romanesque building in Germany. Eight German emperors are buried here

▼ Michelstadt

▼ Breuberg Castle

▼ Boulder field in Odenwald

Heidelberg, university town on the Neckar

▲ Old bridge

Sometimes when the fog rises from the Neckar and envelops the old bridge in a thin veil, Heidelberg becomes the most romantic town in Germany. As in a medieval fairy tale, the castle emerges from the haze. Generations of architects tinkered about with it, each adding new gates, wings, facades and sections to the

▼ Holy Ghost church

▼ University

▼ Student prison

building to create a mixture of styles from Gothic to Renaissance. No wonder that the poets of the Romantic era in the early 19th c. discovered Heidelberg for themselves: Hölderlin penned glowing verses, Brentano went carousing with his friends and Eichendorff sat in the Philosophers' Garden and gazed pensively over the river to Königstuhl. When the railway came in 1840, it brought the tourists with it. Europe became enchanted by Heidelberg.

Students had already been there for years. Ruprecht Karl University was founded in 1386 – the oldest in Germany. However, not all students always behaved in the way that was expected of them. Quite a few cheery carousers thus spent the night in prison after giving their lover a serenade at the tops of their voices. "One for all, all for one" Seiffert, Hauschildt and his three fellow students scrawled on the wall of the cell in which they served a sentence from July 2nd-7th 1901. "Naturally, not guilty!!!!!"

▲ Castle

▼ Castle, large barrel

Historic Franconia – land of the Bocksbeutel

▲ Bamberg
▼ Bayreuth

Richard Wagner ▶

What a beer they brew here! And it is not the famous Kulmbacher alone – that spot, it seems, has its own brewery and its unmistakable brand. "Bamberger Rauchbier", for instance, is to be had only in the town's most famous restaurant, "Schleckerla".

▼ Luisenburg rock labyrinth

▼ Aschaffenburg, Pompejanum

▼ Kulmbach

▲ Tüchersfeld

▲ Volkach

▼ Dinkelsbühl, St. Georg

But they also have a wine – and that's excellent, too! A very wide range of vines grow on very different soils. The best have come for over 250 years in the "Bocksbeutel", that flat-sided bottle that looks rather like a canteen, or, as others claim, the scrotum of a bull.

The Franconians are justifiably proud of their traditions. In Dinkelsbühl, the "Kinderzeche" has been celebrated since 1896 in memory of Lore, the daughter of the tower keeper, who in 1632 collected the children of the town around her and went out through the gate with them to implore the Swedes who were besieging Dinkelsbühl to spare their home town. And her plea was granted. In Bayreuth, Wagner had a festival theatre built in 1876. Since then, international celebrities have gone summer after summer to marvel at the "Flying Dutchman" or "Ring of the Nibelungen". And not only around Volkach do the various wine festivals contend with one another.

▼ Dinkelsbühl, Kinderzeche

Court seat Würzburg on the Main

Würzburg was a bishopric from the 8th c., becoming a city of the princely bishops in 1168. From the 12th up to the 18th c., these rulers resided in Marienberg Fortress, which was given

Residence

its current design around 1600. And the princely bishops also gave the city its baroque face and its festive character. In 1719, one of them, Johann Philipp Franz von Schönborn, found life in the citadel too dull. He therefore called in Balthasar Neumann as architect and commissioned him to build a residence that would be unique. It was built between 1720 and 1744. The residence palace became famous mainly on account of its stairwell featuring wide stairs, white stucco and a 600 m² vaulted ceiling, which the painter Giovanni Battista Tiepolo peopled with the gods of Olympus.

▼ Cathedral, St. Kilian

▼ Cloister in Lusamgärtchen

▲ St. Mary's chapel and Haus zum Falken

▲ Käppele ▼ Marienberg Fortress

The Käppele, a pilgrimage church, was also designed by Neumann, but not the St. Mary's chapel in which he is buried. The latter contains sculptures by the inspired sculptor Tilman Riemenschneider, who in 1520 as mayor supported the rebellious peasants against the spiritual authorities and was then brutally tortured. The museum in the fortress has the largest collection of his works in the world.

Over the old bridge another bishop keeps vigil, blessing the land and his steep vineyards – St. Kilian, after all, is patron saint of wine. A propos wine, the 250m long cellar vault of the Juliusspital with its 220 venerable barrels provides the ideal venue for a wine tasting. The wine taverns in the old "Bürgerhöfe" courtyards, which the canons had built for themselves, are on sunny days attractive places for sipping wine. And a rest awakens appetite: for "Schäufele", a crispy piece of meat from shoulder of pork with "roha Kleess", raw potato dumplings. Or Frankish Zwetschgenbahm, smoked beef ham on a crispy slice of bread baked in the oven of a wood-burning stove. And also at night there's no need to go short – the lights in the pubs of the student town of Würzburg do not go out that quickly.

Historic Franconian metropolis of Nuremberg

Every year ... the Christ Child greets us with his golden crown, and we can enjoy the Christmas market with its fragrance of mulled wine and burnt almonds, the strains of "Silent night" and cheerful children's eyes. Nuremberg toys, Nuremberg clocks, Nuremberg gingerbread early made the city rich and famous. Almost all the emperors of the Holy Roman Empire from the 11th to the 16th c. resided in the castle. Within the mighty town walls, Albrecht Dürer painted his "Praying Hands", Peter Henlein invented the watch, Veit Stoss carved the crucifix and the "Angelic Salutation" for the Lorenzkirche and Peter Vischer

▲ Albrecht Dürer house

▼ "The Hare"

◀ Lorenzkirche

cast the grave of St. Sebald.
Nuremberg is stark, stone turned into history – but sometimes a greeting from the world of today provides a cheerful counterpoint. In 1984 "The Marriage-Go-Round" fountain designed by the sculptor Jürgen Weber was erected, creating an immediate sensation: bronze nudes display in six, partially very drastic scenes the ups and downs of normal married life, based on a poem by Hans Sachs, the most famous poet of the 16th c. Hailing from Nuremberg, of course.

▲ Christmas market in front of St. Mary's Frauenkirche with its beautiful fountain

▲ Nuremberg grilled sausages

◀ Tiergärtner Torplatz with Kaiserburg

◀ Heilig-Geist-Spital

▼ Marriage-Go-Round

Rothenburg o. d. Tauber – "The Middle Ages" live on

In the evening when the thousands of daytime visitors have moved on, quietness descends between Klingenbastei and Rödertor. Now the night watchman does his round with a few remaining guests, people sit cosily together tukking into a shoulder of sucking pig and sipping a glass of Riesling, and the most popular of all Germany's little medieval towns once more comes into its own. By the town clock of the councillors' tavern, the former mayor Nusch raises his glass once again and drinks, as General

▲ Markusturm

▼ Crime Museum

▼ Käthe Wohlfahrt's Christmas village

▲ Town hall and councillors' tavern

Tilly demanded, three-quarters of a litre of wine in one draught, thereby saving himself and sparing his town from destruction. In Käthe Wohlfahrt's Christmas village, wooden Christmas pyramid decorations gyrate and hundreds of ornamental balls glitter on the snowy Christmas tree. A final pair of lovers stroll over the Plönlein to look up to the wonderfully preserved half-timbered facades before disappearing hand in hand through Kobolzeller Tor. Then night falls.

▲ Old forge
▼ Plönlein

Between Upper Middle Rhine and Neckar

◀ Karlsruhe Palace ▲ Karlsruhe

▲ Ludwigsburg Palace

Beautiful towns are located here – and great names are connected with them. In Maulbronn, the best preserved medieval monastery north of the Alps, the astronomer Johannes Kepler and the writer Hermann Hesse went to school. Karlsruhe is associated above all with the name of its founder Karl Wilhelm, Margrave of Baden. In 1715, he designed on the drawing board a town of the future: a fan of streets all leading to the palace. "Built like a star, clear and lucid as a mathematical axiom," as Kleist put it. Today, the Baden State Museum

▼ Baden-Baden, spa centre

▲ Tübingen

◀ Heilbronn, art clock on town hall

▲ Bruchsal, palace

▲ Maulbronn Monastery
▼ Bad Wimpfen

exhibits its treasures in the palace. There is also a long list of those who studied, taught or lived in Tübingen: Philipp Melanchton and Eduard Mörike, Carlo Schmid and Walter Jens, Horst Köhler, Hans Küng, Roman Herzog. The poet Hölderlin lived in the Hölderlin Tower from 1801 and died there in a state of mental derangement.

In Baden-Baden, the casino opened in 1838, and 20 years later the first horses galloped over the racing course during the great Iffzeheim racing week. Champagne flowed; the new ladies' millinery creations were compared; there was in fact no end to the list of celebrated guests: the composer Brahms and the painter Courbet, the violinist Paganini and the writer Mark Twain, the statesman Bismarck and the writer Storm, the composer Johann Strauss and the philosopher Nietzsche. And, naturally, when Russians first turned up: Dostoyevsky, Gogol, Tolstoy, Turgenev …

▲ Old palace

State capital Stuttgart

No trace of Swabian miserliness. The counts and dukes of Württemberg saw to it that their capital was built as a spacious and lordly city – and, of course, made sure that their subjects paid for it. So neither an old palace from the 16th c. nor a new one from the 18th c. is lacking. There are no fewer than five state museums, and a handsome palace square of 61 ha was put right in the centre. Does anyone, then, wonder that back in 1956 Stuttgart indulged in the world's first TV tower, 217m high and still a popular vantage point for looking down on the town?

▲ Mercedes Benz Museum
◀ Vineyard

▼ Rosenheim Palace, Bad Cannstatt

▼ Wilhelma, Bad Cannstatt

▲ Schlossplatz

Or that Wilhelma, the zoological-botanical gardens with its 8,000 animals and 5,000 species of plant is the German zoo with the second largest range of species? Or that the state theatre complete with opera house, ballet and theatre continually attracts attention with prestigious presentations?

Even these days no one thinks of being stingy. The glass cube of the Art Museum displaying the most important collection of the works of Otto Dix was opened in 2005. Mercedes-Benz and Porsche have built ultra-modern car palaces. And a very new, elegant shopping arcade has been built behind the 135m long colonnades of the Königsbau.

Moreover, the locals, incidentally, do not tend, as is always maintained, to be exaggeratedly thrifty. The Cannstadter Wasen, the largest public festival in the region, certainly cannot complain about any lack of visitors.

◀ Collegiate church and Schiller monument

▼ Königsbau

Ulm, former imperial town on the Danube

▲ Town hall Albert Einstein ▶
▶ Ulmer Minster

The people of Ulm always liked to be right up front: "Ulm money rules the world", as the saying went in the Middle Ages, when the locals made a fortune with the textile trade. Later there was a tailor who wanted to fly. And landed in the Danube, although his contraption was proved to function perfectly. A Nobel prize winner was born here whose theory of relativity revolutionised physics. The year 1890 was particularly gratifying for the people of Ulm, as this was when they consecrated the tower of their minster: it is 161.53m, the highest church tower in the world. And Ulm also again attracted attention in recent years when "Ulm's new centre" was positioned within the medieval part of the city. The American architect Richard Meier designed a dazzling white Stadthaus complex. The city library's glass pyramid followed in 2004. A department store, a savings bank building and the Weishaupt Art Gallery complete this intrusion of the modern age into the traditional. And everyone declares again: There the Ulmers go again!

Alte Münz and Schiefes Haus ▲

▲ Hohenzollern Castle

Bad Urach ▶

A long narrow ridge runs through Baden-Württemberg. The farmers once called this barren tract of land "Devil's Cranium" because of the stones that rattled during ploughing. Today, the Alb is a natural gem thanks to its caves, waterfalls and broad foot-paths. And over 100 castles and ruins tower over the land.

▼ Lichtenstein Palace
▶ Urach Waterfall
▶ Blaubeuren, Blautopf

The Danube – lifeline of Europe

▲ Donaueschingen, source

▲ Beuron Monastery

Danube breakthrough ▶

Assuming that "The Brigach and Breg send the Danube on its way", and if you count the Breg as the longer source as well, the Danube stretches for a total of 2,888 km and crosses ten countries before pouring into the Black Sea. Soon after its source, it bites its way through the soft limestone in Donaubergland before flowing straight to the east, passing a number of important places. Straubing with its five-spired town tower became

▼ Straubing

▼ Upper Swabian Baroque Route, Zwiefalten

▲ Kelheim, Hall of Fame

Ingolstadt, Cross Gate ▼

▲ Ingolstadt, palace

known for a big tragic love story: on October 12th 1435, Agnes Bernauer, the beloved of Duke Albrecht III of Munich, was drowned by the people as punishment for venturing to marry above her station. High above Kelheim stands the Hall of Liberation, which Ludwig I had built to commemorate those who fell in the wars of liberation against Napoleon. It acommodates 34 marble goddesses of victory. Finally, Weltenburg Monastery is Bavaria's oldest monastery and also boasts the oldest monastic brewery in the world. Here the Danube battles its way a second time through the rocks into the open.

▼ Weltenburg Monastery

Regensburg – UNESCO world cultural heritage

▲ Stone bridge, bridge gate and cathedral of St. Peter

The 310m long stone bridge leads over the Danube and into the city, which has all the elements of a medieval metropolis with its magnificent Gothic cathedral, the Benedictine monastery of St. Emmeran and a town hall dating from the 14th c. complete with torture chamber. However, it was only in the mid-19th c. that Walhalla was built, modelled on the Parthenon of antiquity. Ludwig I, who commissioned the building, had in mind a meeting of the intellectuals and historical figures "of German tongue" – including those who were active abroad. Between coloured marble walls there are 128 marble busts, from Heinrich I to Sophie Scholl. There are 65 plaques representing figures whose actual appearance is unknown, such as Hermann the Cheruscan. Or the nameless members of the resistance in the Third Reich. There are a mere eleven women among those thus honoured. But that could change, as newcomers can also join. The most recent additions are Carl Friedrich Gauss, the mathematician, Edith Stein, the nun of Jewish origin murdered in Auschwitz, and Heinrich Heine, the great satirist.

▼ Walhalla, Hall of Fame and Honour

▲ Three-river town Passau

Like a pointed tongue, the peninsula "licks" out into the water. The "green" Inn flows from the right and the "blue" Danube from the other side, and from the far left the black Ilz also pushes its way in: Passau is the "three-river town". There are steep steps up to the Stephansdom, the largest baroque cathedral north of the Alps with the world's largest cathedral organ comprising 17,774 pipes resounding, thundering, booming and purring. Popes, kings, the woodcutter from the Bavarian Forest and the BMW manageress from Munich 90 km away have all come to Altötting some time or other. In the Chapel of Mercy, they prayed to the "Black Madonna", in front of whom a drowned child was miraculously restored to life in 1489. And 2,000 votive tablets claim "Mary helped" – for exams, operations, marital problems and sons at war.

Altötting, Kapellplatz ▶

▲ Black Madonna

Fugger town Augsburg

▲ Town hall with Perlachturm

Money was at home here in the 15th and 16th c. – pots of money. The merchants, the Fuggers and Welsers, had grown rich thanks to the cloth and metal trade and gladly lent their capital to kings, princes and hard-up towns. Money made more money. At the beginning of the 16th c., Elias Holl was commissioned to build a town hall that became one of the most beautiful Renaissance buildings of them all. Germany's first council estate was also built here. The local poor – according to the Catholic faith – were allowed to live for as good as nothing in the 67 little Fuggerei houses. However, they had to pray once a day for the founders. Ironically enough, Bert Brecht, the dramatist and vigorous opponent of capitalism, was also born in Augsburg.

◀ St. Ulrich and Afra

▼ Fuggerei

Munich, state capital of Bavaria

This is the home of a cosy, easygoing lifestyle and the football club FC Bayern. BMW belongs to the Bavarian state capital no less than the Föhn wind, the inspectors Batic and Leitmayer of the TV detective series “Tatort” and the grave of Rudolph Moshammer. Munich is known for its film studios, beer gardens, Germany’s largest university and Deutsches Museum with the world’s largest permanent exhibition on science and technology. The turquoise onion domes of the Frauenkirche, consecrated in 1494, are the city’s symbol. No building in the city centre is allowed to be higher than its towers. The new town hall, built between 1867 and 1908 on Marienplatz, is an eye-catcher with its width of 100m and filigree, neo-Gothic style. At noon, the knights, musicians and also the figures of the Shepherds’ Dance, commemorating the end of the plague years, gyrate in the Glockenspiel. In gratitude for the happy end to the Swedish occupation in the 17th c., Maximilan I erected the Mariensäule, which gave the square its name. Wherever you look, Munich is lively and colourful – preferably in the traditional colours of blue and white.

▲ Glockenspiel on town hall
▼ Frauenkirche and town hall

▲ BMW World

▲ Olympiapark

Munich is both ultra-modern and deeply traditional. In the Hofbräuhaus, Japanese women from Kyoto taking snapshots sit next to bearded "locals" clad in leather trousers. On the Viktualienmarkt, there is an amazing selection of fresh saltwater fish, not to mention the classic couple of white sausages served with a pretzel.

In the boutiques in Maximilianstrasse, traditional jackets and felt hats hang alongside the season's latest fashions from Milan. Every time you come to Munich you can expect something new. A visit to the "Musäum" of the Munich "institution" Karl Valentin is still a "must", like a walk in the English Garden, an opera evening in the National Theatre and a visit to some of the many first-rate museums.

▲ Viktualienmarkt
▼ Hofbräuhaus

▲ English Garden

▲ Nymphenburg Palace

On today's programme, however, there's a guided tour over the roof of the Olympia stadium, built for the 1972 Olympics. There's also a big new aquarium on the Olympics site. In the BMW World, the car makers turn the simple act of buying a car into a high-tech experience.

The Oktoberfest, however, is both age-old (since 1810) and getting more packed, noisier and more glamorous year by year. The key data today are as follows. 14 big tents. Approx. 6 million visitors. Some five million litres of beer. The

▲ Group in traditional costume posing in front of the old town hall

Italians have their special day, the groups wearing traditional folk costume march in procession on the first Sunday, and the mayor is judged according to how many blows he needs to open the first barrel. "O'zapft is!" ("It's tapped!") – yes, where has she got to then, the girl in the dirndl, the one carrying liquid Munich gold in the stein?

▲ Oktoberfest

The Black Forest – unspoilt nature and age-old tradition

▲ Triberg Waterfall

How about this Black Forest primer: 1. The first cuckoo clock was built in 1854, designed by a Karlsruhe professor of architecture. Clocks were, admittedly, already being made a century earlier. Clock-making, glass-blowing and agriculture – that's how the local people made a living. 2. The colour of the balls on the "bulb hat" worn with traditional folk costume tells you all really need to know: black means married, red that the Black Forest girl is still single. Although you can't always be so sure nowadays. 3. The Black Forest cherry gateau is made of dark dough, sour cherries, lots of

▼ Hinterzarten

▼ Feldberg

▲ Hexenloch mill

▼ Mummelsee

cream and chocolate chips and a good tot of kirschwasser. Best privately distilled. If you like it less sweet, serve it straight. Best after a hearty Black Forest snack of ham on farmer's bread. 4. The name "Black Forest" naturally comes from the thousands of firs and pines in the highest of Germany's low mountain ranges, not from Professor Brinkmann's "Black Forest Clinic" of TV fame.

University town Freiburg in Breisgau

▲ Minster "Unserer Lieben Frau"

"Z`Friburg in der Stadt, sufer isch´s und glatt," penned the poet Johann Peter Hebel. Yes, it is clean, and that's thanks to the "Bächle", channels in the pavement through which the water merrily murmurs. Once serving as waste water channels, they are now a unique symbol of the city. Freiburg is the southernmost town in Germany – when it comes to joie de vivre. Visitors from all over the world bask in the sun on Münsterplatz, dominated by the 116m perforated spire of the church. Construction of the church began in 1200 and was already finished by 1530 – an achievement by no means to be taken for granted in the Middle Ages. In the evening, students sit on the square Augustinerplatz and make music, the night air is mild, and the sound of Spanish, Japanese and Baden dialect is to be heard all around. The Breisgau is only a few km away. The former volcano is 16 km long and up to 12.5 km wide. In the sunken lanes and on the dry lawns green lizards, bee-eaters and hoopoos live, pasque-flowers and 36 orchid varieties bloom, and you can look far over Markgräfler Land into Alsace and the Vogeses.

▼ Historic department store

▲ Titisee

How about a morning leap into the cool water, a good breakfast in one of the attractive cafes of Titisee and then an excursion to the open-air museum Vogts farm in Gutach. The latter's old farmhouses from different regions of the Black Forest give a vivid picture of local life during the last 400 years. And they are by no means the only large farmsteads with the lowslung roofs typical of the area. There's the Hotzenwaldhaus (1756), in which the weavers sat and ruined their eyes, and the Schnefler workshop, where farmers earned a little on the side in winter by carving spoons and bowls. In the tiny day-labourer's house, the cups are still standing and the hand towels hanging where they were left in 1933. Timber naturally played an important role in the Black Forest the trunks split by knock and drop saw were charred in a pile to make charcoal. There are fields of emmer, unicorn and spelt, while over 130 medicinal herbs flourish in the garden – it was a long way to the doctor in those days, and only a few could afford the treatment. There are beehives, an oil mill, the hemp rubber – the locals had to know how to make use of all the fruits of the earth and the forest if they wanted to survive in a remote area.

▼ Gutach, Vogtsbauernhof

Lake Constance – the "Swabian Sea"

Germany, Austria and Switzerland share the third largest lake in Europe. Its shores stretching for 273 km are studded with interesting

▲ Birnau baroque church

▼ Unteruhldingen pile dwellings

▼ Reichenau island

▼ Langenargen, Montfort Palace

buildings from many periods, such as the cheerful baroque churches of Birnau and Wasserburg, the Gothic and Romanesque church towers on

▲ Friedrichshafen

the island of Reichenau and the pile dwellings in Unteruhldingen, which even bring the Stone Age back to life. In Langenargen, a little palace in Moorish style keeps watch, in Salem Monastery the halls are resplendent in overwhelming rococo, and everywhere you look you'll come across old winepresses, half-timbered facades and historic bridges of widely varying origin. The present day is very much alive on bustling shore promenades, at merry wine festivals and during the celebrations on the colourful "Fasnacht". But the future beckons, too, when the state-of-the-art "NT" airship glides high above busy Friedrichshafen.

▼ Überlingen

▼ Water-surrounded castle

Lindau and Meersburg

▲ Lindau, port entrance

▲ Lindau in Lake Constance

▲ Meersburg, Obertor ▼ Old Palace

Lindau, located on an island in Lake Constance, has belonged to Bavaria since 1806 – the Bavarian lion down by the harbour leaves no doubt about it! But when the ships of the "white fleet" tie up, there's an almost southern flair on the lakeside promenade – just the right home for the "Dear Augustin", the famous figure in the novel by Horst Wolfram Geissler. The paintings on the old town hall depict scenes from the Imperial Diet that convened in Lindau in 1496. The "Haus zum Cavazzen" is regarded as the most beautiful middle-class house on Lake Constance. Meersburg, the "Sun Cape", was home of the poetess Anette von Droste-Hülshoff, who died in her princely little cottage "Fürstenhäusle" in 1848. The defiant castle with the Dagobertturm makes its presence felt far across the lake, while the largest overshot mill wheel in Germany turns under the Schlossbrücke. The half-timbered houses in Steigstrasse are resplendent with floral decoration, while at night the angular turret of the "Zum Bären" inn, the oldest in the town, lights up at the market square.

Constance and the island of Mainau

◀ Constance, Imperia ▲ Constance, Konzil

Count Lennart Bernadotte realised his dream of an exotic paradise on the flower island of Mainau. Tens of thousands of tulips, dahlias and roses bloom on the terraces; exotic butterflies flit and flutter about in the greenhouses. Constance, on the opposite bank, has played host to emperors and cardinals and a famous Council in the course of its eventful history. Today, students from all over the world keep life colourful around the minster, works by the sculptor Peter Lenk make a talking point and medieval "skyscrapers" and murals recall Constance's great past.

▼ Flower island of Mainau

Allgäu – fascinating mountain world

It's a splendidly colourful picture in autumn when the cows go down to the valley, to Oberstaufen, Maierhöfen, Steibis, back from the mountain pastures, where they have spent the summer. The heavy bells ring in melodious confusion, the herdboys whistle, the Alpine herdsmen clad in their best traditional costume look proudly around. Everything went well this summer, no animal has taken a tumble, so the leading cow may wear a magnificently plaited crown. Alpine horns resound from the surrounding heights, the spectators applaud. Then the festi-

▲ Oberstdorf

Cattle drive ▶

▼ Kempten

▼ St. Coloman

▲ Breitachklamm

▲ Nebelhornbahn

▲ Füssen

val opens and the herdsmen's award ceremony begins: who has grown the finest beard in recent months?

The cows, the milk and the cheese – nutty Emmentaler, piquant mountain cheese, hot Romadour – represent the economic backbone of the Allgäu. Along with the tourists today, who can enjoy an unspoilt natural landscape, exciting ski slopes and attractive towns. Kempten, the Allgäu capital, displays all the magnificence and splendour of its princely episcopal residence. And its museum shows us the transition from the "blue" Allgäu of flax cultivation to the "green" of the dairy industry and of tourism – a long and successful career.

▲ Allgäu cheese dairy

Royal Castle Neuschwanstein

▲ Neuschwanstein

The dreamer on the throne had a vision. And had it realised in brick and clad in limestone, thus creating in the mid-19th c. a castle that is more artificial than any other, yet with a splendour that overshadows them all. Entering a throne room like a Byzantine church, you pass through marble portals into the wood-panelled hall, which recalls the singers' contest on the Wartburg. The Blue Grotto, an artificial stalactite cave, separates living and working rooms. And everywhere hang curtains of brocade, with walls papered in gold-embroidered silk and displaying frescos of troubadours and heroes from the remote past: Tannhäuser, Lohengrin, Parzifal. However, behind the scintillating surface the most advanced technology of the 19th c. is skilfully concealed: flush toilets, a dumb waiter and an electric call system.

◀ King Ludwig II

▲ Wieskirche

▲ Wieskirche, ceiling fresco

But Ludwig II "recreated" more than the Middle Ages. He was also enthralled by baroque and rococo. Which is why Linderhof Palace was built at the same time – even more colourful, glittering and overflowing with silver chandeliers and furniture with lion's feet adorning the rooms, stucco climbing and winding over the walls and the Hall of Mirrors dazzling in blue, white and gold. In the park, a 30-step cascade splashes away, a fountain shoots up to 22 metres into the air, and a gold-plated shell-shaped boat glides through the Venus Grotto.

The baroque neighbour is, no doubt about it, the more splendid edifice. At the beginning of the 18th c., the farmer's wife Maria Lori had seen tears in the shimmering eyes of the chastised Saviour in the nearby monastery. Henceforth it attracted crowds of pilgrims, and eventually the monastery authorities commissioned Dominikus Zimmermann to build a church there between 1745 and 1754. "The Wies," noted the author Peter Dörfler, "is a piece of heaven on this woebegone earth." Be that as it may, it's certainly the most beautiful of all rococo churches, a hall flooded with light, a Christian riot in white and gold. And the thousands of votive tablets testify that faith in the power of the picture is still unbroken.

▼ Linderhof Palace

Upper Bavaria – mountains, lakes and a traditional way of life

Life here has a rustic flavour, so quite a few old customs have been preserved to the present day. In spring, the local young people set up the maypole and try to steal the one in the neighbouring village, which then has to "redeemed" with plenty of beer. In Holy Week, the locals cut palm leaves and hang them over the altar pictures in the church. On Corpus Christi, the entire parish goes through blooming meadows to

▲ Walchensee ▼ Alpspitze in Werdenfelser Land

▼ Church in Ramsau

▲ Sylvenstein Lake

flower-bedecked altars, in their midst the priest carrying the monstrance under a brocade heaven of a canopy, borne by four important local men. In autumn, the countryfolk don their precious traditional folk costumes, plait the horses' manes and take off in their horse-drawn wagons for the Leonhardi pilgrimages.

And things really get going at the country fair! The music for wind instruments sounds forth, on the stage fingertuggers test their strength, schuhplattlers revolve, the boys outdo one another cracking their whips, and whether a fellow really is a fine figure of a man is shown quite simply by the size of the tuft of chamois hair on his hat.

▲ Andechs Monastery

▼ Starnberger See

◀ Maypole

▼ Bad Tölz

Oberammergau and Ettal

In 1633, the plague was raging all about. In their plight, the citizens of Oberammergau vowed to perform a "play about the agony, death and resurrection of our Lord Jesus Christ" every ten years if nobody else was struck down. The first performance was at Whitsun 1634. And since then, the community discusses every ten years who is to play the Saviour and who Mary. Apart from the festivals, the local wood-carvers also account for Oberammergau's fame.

In the "Living workshop" in the Pilatushaus we can see how figures of Mary, bellowing stags and the hunter Jennerwein take shape under the craftsmen's hands.

▲ Oberammergau, Pilate's House

▲ Oberammergau, Passion play ▼ Ettal Monastery

Zugspitze and Garmisch-Partenkirchen

▲ Zugspitze, cross on summit

▲ Zugspitze, Münchner Haus

You can't get any higher anywhere else in Germany. The 2,966m Zugspitze is the peak of peaks. However, you don't necessarily have to climb it on foot. A cog railway leads up from Partenkirchen, and there is also a cableway. On clear days, at the summit you get a view of Bernina, Grossvenediger, the Dolomites and Munich, the highest internet connection in Germany and the highest church. In which you can, of course, pinnacle of joy, also marry. In the valley below, the descendants of Matthias Klotz, who learned his craft with Stradivari, still make their violins. And in the Partnachklamm the howling of the wind and the rushing of the water create their own harsh music.

▼ Garmisch-Partenkirchen

▼ Mittenwald with Karwendel

▼ Partnachklamm

Herrenchiemsee, Fraueninsel and Bad Reichenhall

Versailles was the model for Ludwig II when he set about building Herrenchiemsee. And it is certainly fitting that the magnificent stairwell bears his name. What is described here as "anteroom" would be considered a splendidly ornate chamber anywhere else. Ludwig's 98m long large mirror gallery is even larger than that of the Sun King. And whenever he felt like it, the young king could take his meals without having any servants around: at his command, a richly laden magic table rose from the floor. In Bad Reichenhall, a voyage of discovery into salt awaits us. We descend via the historic chute into the old saltworks of 1834, which once made the town rich. The former brine conduit with the pump is still there today. In the salt cathedral, salt laboratory and mirror lake, an impressive multimedia show depicts the creation of the "white gold" and how it was extracted.

▼ Bad Reichenhall, old saltworks

▼ Bad Reichenhall, Gradierhaus

▲ Lookout point Jenner

▲ Berchtesgaden with Watzmann

Softly a song resounds over the Königssee, echoes off the snow-covered flank of the Watzmann, over which a solitary eagle circles, and carries across to St. Bartholomä, where the fisherman takes whitefish out of the smoke, plays around the boatsheds with their hip roofs, where the old artist is at work ... and dies away ...

▼ Königssee

Kehlstein peak ▶

GERMANY

... at a glance!

Founded on:	January 18th 1871 German Empire – May 23rd 1949 Federal Republic of Germany (Basic Law) October 7th 1949 - Founding of the GDR October 3rd 1990 - German reunification
National public holiday:	October 3rd (Day of German Unity)
Area:	357,092 sq km
Population:	82,258 million
Capital:	Berlin, 3.4 million inhabitants
Form of government:	Democratic-parliamentary federal state
Federal states:	16 – Baden-Württemberg, Bavaria, Berlin, Brandenburg, Bremen, Hamburg, Hesse, Mecklenburg-West Pomerania, Lower Saxony, North Rhine-Westphalia, Rhineland-Palatinate,Saarland, Saxony, Saxony-Anhalt, Schleswig-Holstein, Thuringia
Currency:	1 euro = 100 cents
Neighbouring countries:	Belgium, Denmark, France, Luxemburg, Netherlands, Austria, Poland, Switzerland, Czech Republic
Highest mountain:	Zugspitze, 2,962 metres
Longest rivers (navigable):	Rhine 865 km, Elbe 700 km, Danube 647 km, Main 524 km, Weser 440 km, Saale 427 km, Spree 382 km, Ems 371 km, Neckar 367 km, Havel 343 km, Werra 292 km, Mosel 242 km, Fulda 218 km, Elde 208 km, Oder 162 km
Largest lakes:	Lake Constance 572 sq km, Müritz 110 sq km, Chiemsee 80 sq km, Schweriner See 61 sq km, Starnberger See 56 sq km
Population density:	231 inhabitants per sq km
Official language:	German (most spoken native language in the EU)

Dear reader,
SCHÖNING-VERLAG would like to thank you for having purchased our product.
We know that you will enjoy it as a travel guide and souvenir.
Please don't hesitate to contact us if you have any suggestions or queries. These travel guides have been published on many German towns, cities and regions, and many of them have been translated into other languages.
We are continually expanding the series. Please also visit our website: www.schoening-shop.de